P9-CST-487
North Pole
Arctic Ocean
Atlantic Ocean
North America
Ocean
Pacific
Equator
South America
Antarctic Ocean
South Pole
of World
Western Hemisphere

George Matthies

28 Peace St.,

Seymour, Conn.,

JAPANESE CHILDREN LIKE TO FEED THE SACRED DEER IN THE PARK.

LITTLE FOLKS OF OTHER LANDS

By

WATTY PIPER

ILLUSTRATED BY

LUCILLE W. and H. C. HOLLING

·NEW·YORK·

·THE·PLATT·&·MUNK·CO INC·

MADE IN U. S. A.

CONTENTS

TO THE BOYS AND GIRLS WHO WILL READ THIS BOOK

You all want to cross the ocean in a big steamship, I'm sure. Perhaps some of you are looking forward to going by air some day.

But there is an easier way to travel than that. It is the book way. Without the trouble of packing even an over-night bag, this book will take you to many far away and fascinating lands. Watty Piper hopes that it will do more than that.

One of the pleasantest things about going to new places is making new friends, isn't it? The little folks from far away, whom you will meet in these pages, do not wear clothes like yours. They do not eat the same kind of food. But under their skins, you will find they are not so different from you after all. Surely you can be friends.

And now we're off. A pleasant journey.

WATTY PIPER.

LITTLE FOLKS FROM THE LAND OF CHERRY BLOSSOMS

Have you ever looked at the dainty china, the decorated screens and fans, the beautiful paintings, cards and prints in a shop where Japanese goods are sold? On all these things Japanese artists have pictured chrysanthemums, cherry blossoms, queer twisted trees, and snowy topped mountains shaped like great ice-cream cones.

The Japanese love all these things that belong to the out-of-doors so much that they want them in their pictures. They may well be proud of their land, for they have one of the most beautiful countries on the other side of the globe.

Their country is made up of a chain of hundreds of islands, a chain twisting like a great snake through the Pacific Ocean for two thousand miles. If the land in all these islands were put together, there would be about as much of it as there is in our own state of California. Over fifty million people live in these beautiful islands.

There is no country in the world where you could see more different kinds of beauty. Your Japanese friends admire their flowers so much that they have named different seasons of the year for the time when they blossom. There are the plum and cherry blossom season in the spring, the chrysanthemum and maple season in the fall.

When the cherry trees bloom, everybody takes a holiday and goes to the parks to enjoy their pinkness. The boys and girls carry their luncheons in gay colored handkerchiefs. They picnic under the trees or go into the tea houses for rice cakes and tea. Everyone likes to feed the sacred deer kept in the parks.

The Japanese love their snow-capped mountains and most of all Fujiyama, their sacred mountain. Many pilgrims who wish to make themselves more holy climb to the top every year. Fujiyama is more than twice as high as our own Mount Washington in the White Mountains. Long ago it used to send out from its top clouds of smoke and melted rock, for it was a volcano.

The boys and girls who live in this beautiful land are polite, good-

natured young folks. Their skin is not white like yours, but light yellow. Like the Chinese, they belong to the Yellow Race. Their eyes do not open as widely as yours, which makes them appear to be slanting.

Little Miss Yuki San wears her jet black hair long. Her older sister and her mother comb theirs up in rolls on the top of their heads. They often have a hairdresser arrange it for them. They are very careful not to muss their beautiful rolls and puffs at night.

Yuki San's dress is a long kimono made of pretty figured cotton. It is folded over in front and held in place by a wide sash called an obi. She can use her long loose sleeves for pockets. Her best kimono, the one she wears in cherry blossom time, is of gaily figured silk.

Yuki San never wears a hat. Instead she carries a bright colored umbrella of oiled paper to keep off sunshine or showers. You wonder how Yuki San can walk in her strange shoes. They are like sandals held on by thongs that pass between the big toe and the next one. In rainy weather her shoes are set up on two little strips of wood to keep them out of the mud. She looks as if she were walking on stilts. Yuki San, like all polite little Japanese girls, always leaves her shoes at the door. Many little Japanese girls no bigger than five years old, carry a baby brother or sister on their backs when they go out to play.

Togo, Yuki San's brother, wears a kimono, also, but his is narrower than his sister's and it has a narrower belt. Both boys and girls in Japan are dressed very much like the grown-ups. Cotton is worn for everyday and silk for best. The Japanese raise silkworms and make very beautiful silks and satins.

Of course, you want to visit Togo's home. You can see a great deal of a Japanese house without going inside. In the morning the heavy outside shutters are slid wide open. The partitions between the rooms are made of paper. The family divide the house into as many rooms as they like by sliding the paper partitions back and forth.

The house seems very bare to us at first. Where are the chairs, the tables, beds, rugs and ornaments? Togo and Yuki San sit on cushions instead of chairs. The only ornament is a beautiful vase holding a spray of cherry blossoms. It stands on a platform in front of a picture of Fujiyama. Yuki San takes lessons in arranging flowers. Like every Japanese house, this one has its little shrine. Every day offerings of food are set there for the gods.

Yuki San takes you to the beautiful garden with its tiny bridges and stone lanterns, and shows you the little building where the household treasures are kept. In Japan the land often trembles and shakes. The little houses with their paper partitions catch fire very easily so the family keeps the things they treasure most in a fireproof house called a godown.

The children's mother invites you to stay for dinner. Togo and his sister make a low bow to their parents as they seat themselves at the long, low table. The housemaid kneels down and bows low as she brings in the trays of food. Some of the food is all ready to eat, and the rest of it is prepared on the table over a little charcoal stove, during the meal.

If you were to spend the night in this Japanese home, one of the maids would slide aside a screen door and bring out from a cupboard some pads and comforters. These she would spread on the matting floor and small wooden blocks would be used for pillows.

There is a nice little bathroom in Togo's and Yuki San's house, for the Japanese are very clean and like to bathe often.

Your mother would scold if you ate your soup as noisily as these children do, but in Japan it is thought good manners to make a loud sucking noise when eating soup. After their soup which was made of seaweed and fish, they have more fish, some of it raw, roast eels, vegetables and plenty of rice served in round wooden buckets.

Like the Chinese people, the Japanese raise a great deal of rice. They are also famous for their fine tea. It is served at Togo's house without cream or sugar in tiny cups just about the right size for a dolls' tea party. You would like best of all the meal, the rice cakes, odd candies and sugared plums.

Yuki San wants to show you her dolls that are kept safely put away in the godown. She has hundreds of them. Some have belonged in her family for many years. On the third of March, which is the Feast of Dolls, she gets them all out. Then for two or three days, what fun she and the other little girls have dressing and undressing the old and new dolls, giving tea parties and playing house!

Togo thinks the boys' festival in May is better. Then all the boys have presents of flags and toys. They fly kites and play games. They fight sham battles with wooden swords and pretend they are defending the Emperor. Japan has an Emperor instead of a President like ours.

Togo and Yuki San coax you to stay longer and visit their school. The Japanese have very fine schools and every child has to go. They would take you riding too, in a high two-wheeled carriage, called a jinrikisha, drawn by a little brown man.

How hard it is to say sayonara, which means good-bye in Japanese, to such an interesting country as Japan and to such pleasant little companions as slant-eyed Togo and Yuki San!

LITTLE FOLKS FROM THE LAND OF WINDMILLS

Did you ever hear of a country where the boats skimming along on the ocean are higher up than the boys and girls walking in the streets? Where the children would have to climb to the second story of their house to be on a level with these boats?

It sounds like a make-believe place, but ocean steamers are leaving our ports nearly every day for this country where the land in many of its parts is lower than the sea. The Netherlands, which means low lands, is one name for this country. Another name is Holland.

But I know you want to say: "Why doesn't the water come in and cover the country all up, if the land is so low?" It would have long ago if the people had not built high broad walls called dikes to keep it out. (The diagram on the next page shows how this was done.)

For many, many years the Dutch people have been playing a kind of game with the ocean to see which should have the land. This is the way it began. They took a little piece of swampy land and built walls around it. Then they built windmills to pump up the water into canals. The canals carried the water away to the ocean. Then they built ditches to drain off more water. By and by their piece of land was dry enough to hold houses. Then they did the same thing to another piece of land. They kept on doing this until they had enough land to make one of the finest little countries in Europe.

To be sure, it is a very small country (15,760 square miles) only as large as our own state of Maryland. It has over seven and a half million inhabitants, about five times as many people as Maryland.

But to make even so small a country meant a great deal of patient work. It is work that has to be kept up, for the ocean is always trying to get into this tidy green land that the Dutch took away from it. Especially in winter the ocean lashes its waves against the walls and tries to tear holes in them.

The Hollanders keep a guard on the dikes day and night. If the ocean forces its way in, they ring an alarm. Then everybody comes to help mend the dike.

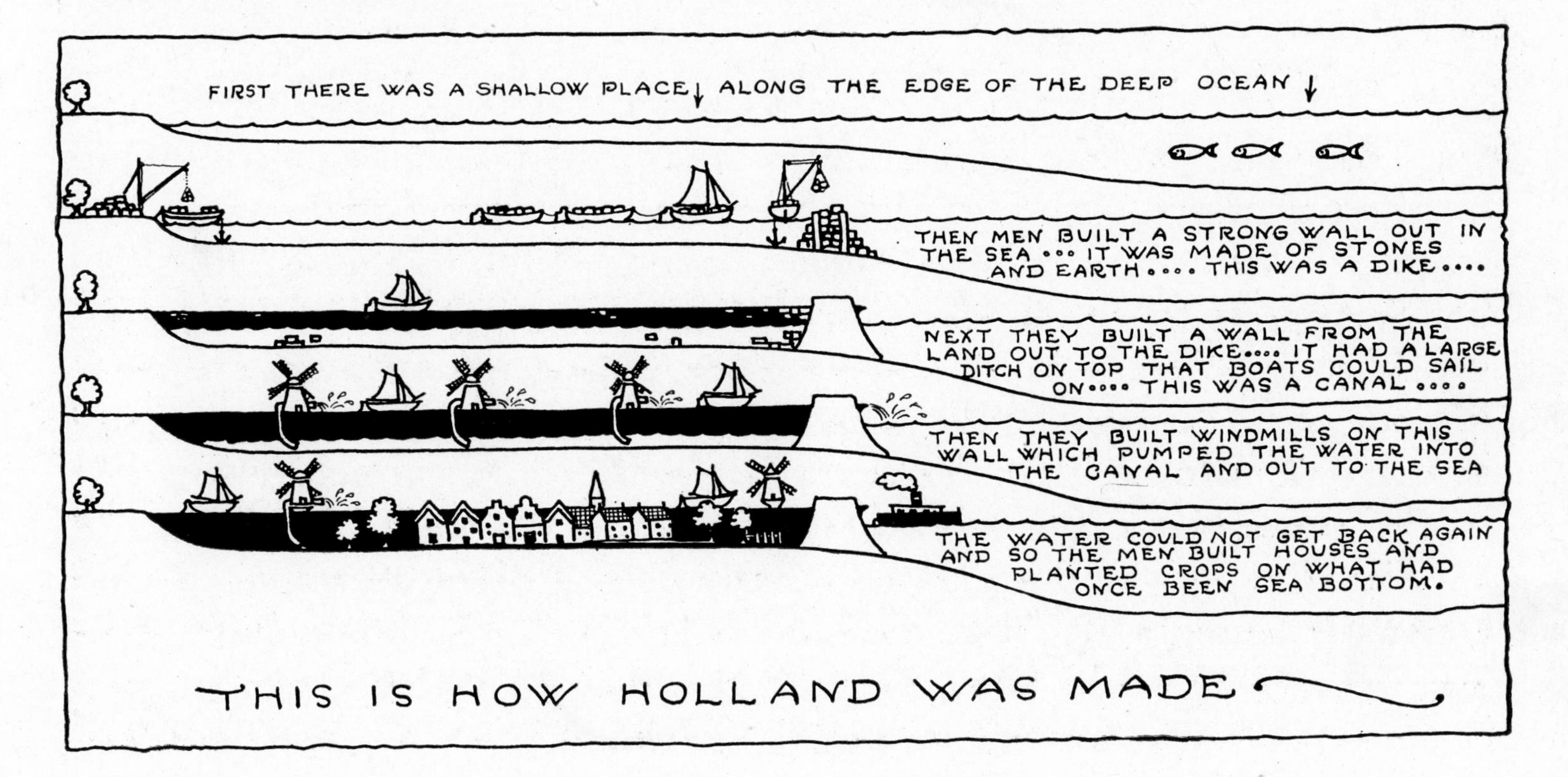

THIS IS HOW HOLLAND WAS MADE

The people of Holland have had to build a great many of these dikes. If they were all placed together and set down in our own United States, you might go from Boston away across the country into Nebraska on their tops. You might ride in an automobile, for they are wide enough for two cars to pass.

In Holland the dikes are often the favorite strolling places for the people. Let us pretend that we are walking along in the midst of the crowd all dressed up in their holiday best. What a clatter they make with their wooden shoes on the stone paving of the dike.

They are strong healthy looking people. But what strange clothes!

Don't laugh at the baggy trousers, short coats and wide-brimmed caps that the men wear. The women look odd to us, too. Their skirts are so very wide and full and they wear so many of them. But their caps of dainty muslin and lace are very pretty. You can see the glitter of gold, silver or brass underneath. Some have ornaments of metal at each side. A Dutch woman is very proud of her undercap or helmet, especially if it is of gold, Often it belonged to her grandmother and great-grandmother before her and she will give it to her own little girl.

As for the little folks, they look like small editions of their fathers and mothers, for they are dressed just the same. In cities and large towns, you will see many Dutch people in clothes like your own, but in many parts of Holland the Dutch like to wear the same kind of clothing that their ancestors have been wearing for centuries.

Wouldn't it be fun to go home with one of these rosy-cheeked Dutch boys and girls? This blue-eyed, flaxen-haired little girl is called Wilhelmina. Her brother's name is Pieter, or Piet for short. Wilhelmina, like many other little Dutch girls, was named for Queen Wilhelmina of the Netherlands. Queen Wilhelmina rules Holland with the help of a congress called the States General which the people choose themselves. Really you see, the Dutch people have almost as much to say about the running of their country as we do. Queen Wilhelmina lives in the capital city called The Hague.

Our little Wilhelmina's house is built close to a canal. She often goes out on her front steps to watch her father sailing off to carry his butter and cheese to market.

There are many, many canals in Holland, two thousand miles of them, some big and some little. They are to Holland what roads and streets are to us. In the winter time the canals freeze over and then, more than ever they are alive. Everybody puts on skates with runners that turn up like a swan's neck, and they go gliding over the long smooth stretches of ice. Wilhelmina and Brother Piet skate to school and their father skates to market.

As we near Wilhelmina's home, we look up at the red-tiled roof. A queer long-legged bird is perched on a nest of sticks on the chimney. It is a stork. The Dutch people are always kind to storks for they eat the frogs and worms which make holes in the dikes. The Dutch like to think that the stork brings good luck.

At the door step Wilhelmina stops and takes off her clumsy wooden shoes. No polite Dutch person ever thinks of wearing soiled shoes into the spickness and spanness of a Dutch house. How everything shines and glistens as we step into the long low room. Even the heavy wooden chairs and tables are washed once a week. The tiled floor is mopped and scrubbed every day. The rows of blue plates on the mantel are never allowed to gather a bit of dust. In fact so neat a housekeeper is Wilhelmina's mother that every day she washes down the front of the house with a mop on the end of a long pole.

LITTLE WILHELMINA'S HOUSE IS BUILT CLOSE TO A CANAL.

We do not see any bedrooms in Wilhelmina's house, but she opens a door in the wall and shows us her bed in the closet. It looks very much like a berth in a stateroom except that it has curtains of bright colors.

We notice another odd thing about this Dutch house. Outside each window hangs a narrow mirror at right angles to the wall. By looking in it we can see the people passing when they are some distance away. Wilhelmina's mother, while she sits knitting, can see her neighbors coming or watch for the children getting home from school.

But we must bid good-bye to Wilhelmina and Piet if you are to see more of their tidy little country. If you could climb into a low flying airplane, you would have a fine view. Let us pretend we can. How very flat the country is. There isn't a mountain or even a hill. This flat country looks a little like a great green checkerboard divided off by its many ditches and canals.

In the green fields there are black and white Holstein cows grazing contentedly. The Dutch take very good care of their cows. They give them plenty to eat and keep them in comfortable, clean quarters. Of course such cows as these give a great deal of good rich milk. The farmer saves some of the milk and also sells some to the dairies. The dairies with the help of machinery can turn it into butter and cheese much more quickly than the farmer could by hand. The Dutch are famous for their fine cheese. They are very fond of it themselves, but more than half of what they make is loaded on big steamers at the shipping port of Amsterdam and sent to our own and other countries.

Everywhere we see windmills, for nearly every farmer has one. The wind that blows so steadily off the ocean whirls their great sails round and round. Some of the windmills are pumping water from the fields; others are grinding wheat.

And there we see great fields of gay tulips, their heads nodding in the wind. You can buy big bunches of them in the markets for a few cents, but the bulbs from which they grow are more costly. Sometimes a bulb-grower pays a very large price for a particularly rare kind of bulb. The Dutch are as famous for their bulbs as for their cheeses. The growers care far more for the bulbs than for the flowers.

Now as we look down upon a canal we see men get out on the bank to pull their barges along with ropes. They have to do this when the wind dies down. Sometimes they have a big dog to help. Dogs are expected to earn their keep in Holland. You can often see them on the banks harnessed to milk and vegetable carts.

There are thousands of little Dutch boys and girls who have no other homes but these barges. But they live very happily nevertheless. Often their father keeps a cow on board and the mother has pots of growing flowers. When the children are tired of playing on the decks, they can go ashore and romp along the banks of the canal.

Don't you think that Holland, though so tiny, is a fine little country? I'm sure you will want to get better acquainted with it some day and its sturdy industrious people.

LITTLE FOLKS OF THE DESERT

When you have been playing in the hot sun, nothing tastes quite so good as a drink of cold water. Ahmed and Hada live in a country far, far hotter than ours. Yet when they are thirsty they can have only a sip of luke-warm water from a goat-skin. To reach the nearest well, they must travel miles and miles over the burning sands.

This hot dry land where they live is called Arabia. The sea touches it for four thousand miles, but fresh water is very, very scarce. Arabia has almost no rivers except some which run underground. In some parts of Arabia rain seldom falls, and even the ocean breezes that blow across this big neck of land in western Asia are warm and dry. You wonder why anyone chooses to live in such a place, but about five million people do live there.

Some of the people live in villages in houses of sun-dried brick, but many have no home but a tent. Ahmed and Hada live in a tent made of goat-skin. It is broad and low and has two rooms, one for Hada and her mother, and the other for Ahmed and his father. Sometimes Ahmed's beautiful horse, Selim, wanders into the tent too, and makes himself quite at home.

THE ARABS ARE VERY FOND OF THEIR HORSES.

Ahmed's father Hassan, owns many horses. They are smaller than our horses, but beautifully formed. They can travel a long time without needing a drink. The Arabs are very fond of their horses and treat them like members of the family.

Ahmed does not always ride on his horse. Sometimes he rides on a camel. Although Father Hassan has no house, he is a rich man. He owns many camels besides his horses and flocks of sheep and goats. He is a chief, too, which means that he rules over his tribe.

But how can Father Hassan's animals get enough to eat in so dry and sandy a country? This is the reason. Arabia is not all desert. There are green spots here and there where the cattle can graze. When they have eaten the grass in these places, the family must move on.

The camel with his hump in the middle of his back is the most useful of all Father Hassan's animals. The camel can carry a heavy load for miles over the desert. He has a convenient kind of stomach in which he can store away enough food and drink to last a week. His broad feet keep him from sinking into the sand.

When moving time comes, the camels kneel down and the servants load them with the tents and the family belongings. Some of the people ride on the camels and some on horseback.

Often the family sleep during most of the day, and travel by the light of the stars in the cooler night air. At meal time, it is polite for the men to eat first. Each person has a piece of flat bread that he uses for a plate. Ahmed dips up his stew from the pot with this piece of bread. There are not many dishes to wash after a desert meal, because everybody eats up his plate. After dinner, Father Hassan drinks many cups of coffee and smokes his long pipe. The children have camel's milk to drink. Everybody eats dates, even the horses, camels and dogs.

Let us look at our Arab friends as they sit on the sand beside their tent. They have black hair and deeply set black eyes. Their skin has been darkened by the sun, but they belong to the white race.

The children wear loose cotton clothing. When they were smaller, they wore none at all. Father Hassan has a cloak of camel's hair. Over his head he wears a piece of silk which hangs down over his shoulders. Ahmed's mother keeps her face covered, all but her eyes.

Ahmed and Hada are always very glad when they see trees in the distance. They know that they are coming to a grassy spot called an oasis. The trees are date palms with leaves like great plumes at the top. The sweet dates grow in clusters below the leaves.

The Arabs could not do without the date tree. They make poles for their tents from its trunk. Of the leaves they weave mats and baskets. But the children think the sweet fruit is the best part of all.

This family of Bedouins, as these wandering tribes are called, sometimes meet pilgrims going to visit the holy city of Mecca where their prophet Mohammed was born. They also meet long trains of camels called caravans. The camel's packs are filled with dates, coffee and wool to be sold to other countries. Sometimes robbers try to steal these goods. Often Father Hassan or some other friendly chief will lend the travelers many men to ride beside them and frighten the thieves away.

There is another danger for travelers in the desert. Often the hot winds blow the sand so fiercely in their faces that they are blinded by it. In a sand storm, the wise camels lie down and push their noses into the cooler sand underneath.

Doesn't it make you feel hot and thirsty to hear about these little folks of the desert?

LEIF AND HELGA HAD MANY A GOOD ROMP ON THEIR FATHER'S SHIP.

LITTLE FOLKS FROM THE LAND OF THE VIKINGS

It seems a very long time ago that Columbus crossed the great uncharted ocean and discovered our own country. But even before that time, there were seamen sailing unknown seas. Most of them in those days thought that the earth was flat, and timid sailors kept close to shore for fear of dropping off the edge of the world.

The Norsemen or Viking's however, were more daring. They hoisted the bright sails of their stout ships and boldly turned their dragon-shaped prows toward the open sea. They discovered an island called Iceland and a barren shore called Greenland. And one of them, Leif Ericson, it is said, sailing and rowing by turns, came even as far as America.

We can imagine how exciting the days for setting sail must have been for Viking boys and girls. All winter long they had listened to stories and songs of the sea. With the coming of the spring, their fathers were busy splicing ropes, whittling new oars, and mending sails.

Their mothers were packing great casks with hard rye bread and dried fish. The boys and girls probably helped as much as possible, but as they ran back and forth on errands, sturdy Leif and Helga of the flying flaxen braids had time for many a good romp on their father's ship lying at anchor in the fjord.

There are still blue-eyed, flaxen-haired boys and girls in the land of the Vikings, but now the country is called Norway. The Vikings firmly believed that the giants had used their country as a playground; that they had amused themselves by pulling up the land and letting the sea into it, and by pelting one another with the mountains and islands. The country looks as if that might have been true. Norway is not half as big as our own state of Texas, but if its jagged coast line could be straightened out into one long strip, it would stretch half way around the world at the equator.

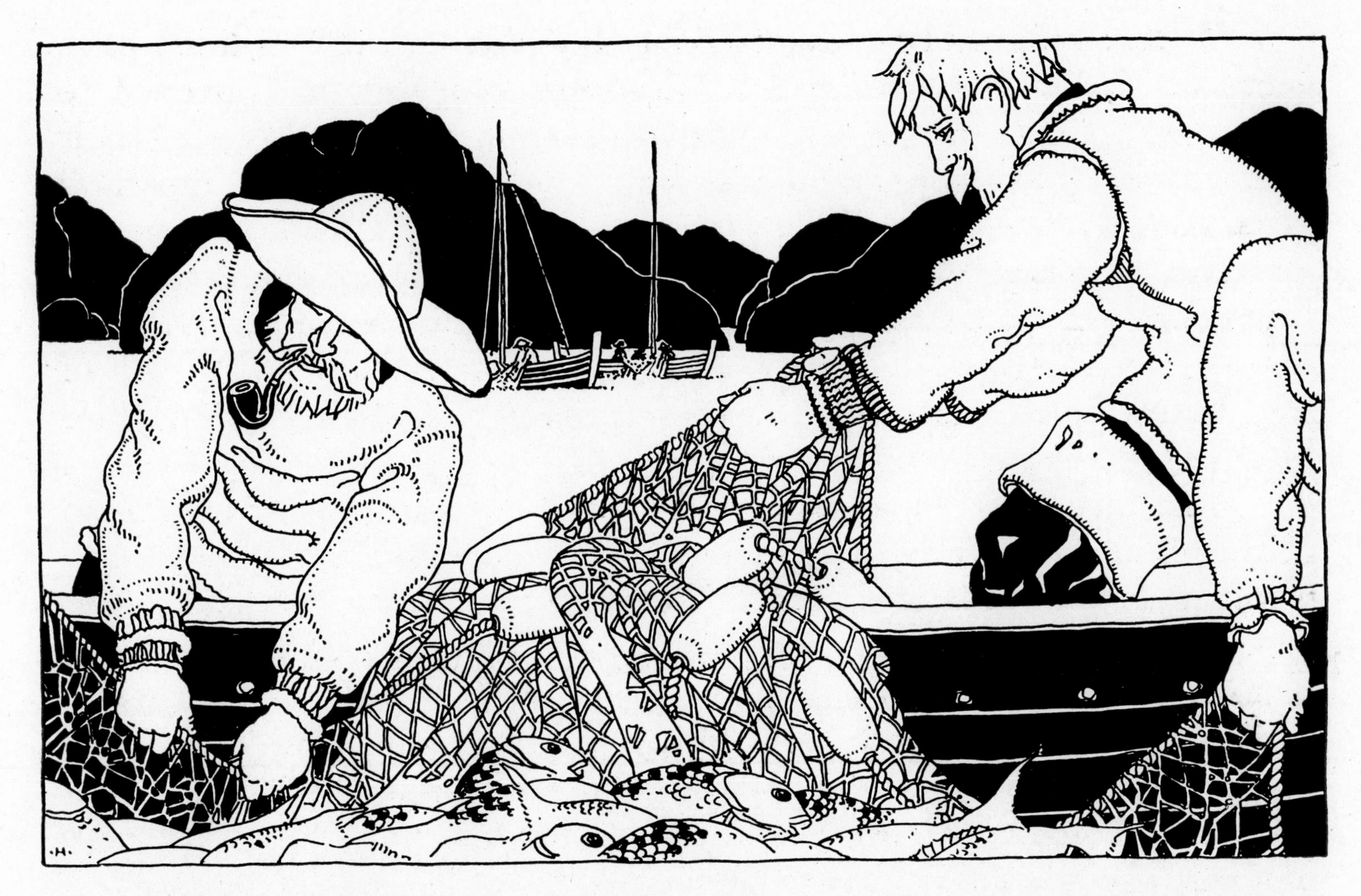

And so packed with beauty is this country that every summer people come from all over the world to admire its deep bays called fjords running sometimes a hundred miles into the land, its snow-capped mountains and the sun shining at midnight as it may be seen in the northerly part of Norway. There are only two million and a half people in Norway, that is fewer people to a square mile than in any other country of Europe.

Like true descendants of the Vikings a great many of these people look to the sea for their living. Ole's father goes fishing for cod. When he tells Ole how the men of his fleet catch three or four hundred silvery cod in their nets and almost as many on their fish lines in a day's haul, the boy coaxes to be taken along. He does not realize what hard work it is to fish in the icy waters. The cod come near the shore in the winter and early spring so those cold seasons make the best fishing time. The fishermen also catch great quantities of mackerel, herring and other fish.

But though many Norwegians spend a great deal of their time on the water, many others get their living from the land. Margit's father has a tiny farm. There are so many mountains in Norway that there is not much good land for farming. That is why the farms have to be small. Margit's father has to raise a great deal of hay to feed his cattle through the long, cold winter. Without his cows there would be no butter, milk or cheese.

Even the hillsides are scraped for every spear of grass. Sometimes a wire is stretched from a high slope down to the valley. Margit's brother Hjalmar ties the hay into bundles and sends them sliding down the wire. In the valley the boys and girls help spread the grass on long poles to dry.

In June all the cows and sheep are sent high up in the mountains. If they stayed in the valley, they would eat up all the good grass and there would be no hay for winter. Margit and her sister Hedda and her younger brother, Haakon, go to spend the summer in their dairy house, called a saeter. They think it good fun to go camping out in this stone hut, but they have little time for play. They have to keep the cattle from straying and call them home by blowing on their birch-bark horns. They make butter and cheese, and in odd moments Margit knits stockings and mittens for winter.

It is lonely up at the saeter, for the home folks are too busy with the haying to make many visits. Hjalmar may get up once or twice with a fresh supply of his mother's flat bread of rye and barley meal, and salted or dried fish. He carries back a load of cheese and perhaps a little bundle of hay.

Margit is glad to go up to the saeter, but she is even more glad to get back home again. After the long lonely summer, she is eager to meet her friends at church. She enjoys the trip across the fjord in the family row-boat and she likes wearing her Sunday clothes. And well she may, for she has one of the prettiest costumes in Norway. Her full blue skirt is covered with a sort of apron finely embroidered. She has a red velvet bodice trimmed with many colored beads and a big silver brooch, once her grandmother's. On her fair, flowing hair, she wears a gaily embroidered cap.

In winter Margit, Haakon and all other little Norwegians and many big ones, skim over the snow on long runners called skis. If you have ever tried to walk on skis, you know how hard it is to keep your balance. But Norwegian boys and girls learn the knack very young. Some of them can take flying leaps into the air and land safely on their feet. They think there is no sport in the world like skiing.

These boys and girls of Norway are proud of the beauty of their country, of its wise government and good schools, of the great men it has given them, and they are proud, too, to be descendants of the brave and hardy Vikings.

LITTLE FOLKS OF THE PUEBLOS

You and I are very likely to think that an apartment house is about the most up-to-date thing in homes. Here is a surprise for you! There were apartment houses in our very own country long before Columbus came over and discovered it.

These apartment houses were in the Southwest, in what is now the states of Arizona and New Mexico, and they are still there. There are people living in them, too. The Spaniards who found these high houses on the cliffs called them pueblos, which means village or town. We call the people who live in them Pueblo Indians.

Little White Dove and her family live in a pueblo built on a rock cliff in the bottom of a red rock canyon. They have a two-room apartment on the second floor. This little girl's grandmother and great-grandmothers years and years ago lived in these same rooms.

Little White Dove has to climb a flight of steps and walk over a neighbor's roof to reach her home. The family on the third floor climb a ladder and walk over Little White Dove's roof to get to theirs. The flat roofs of the houses seem to make a great flight of steps.

Each apartment is built of clay called adobe. At spring-cleaning time, Little White Dove's mother gives the outside walls a fresh coat of yellow mud. The inside she whitewashes neatly.

There is a fireplace in the larger room. The chimney pot is made out of an old jar with the bottom broken out. In the olden days, pueblos had only peep-holes for windows. Now they have real glass. Mother tries to keep the room tidy by hanging the things not in use upon the walls or ceiling.

LITTLE CHIPMUNK COMES RIDING WITH A DOLL FOR LITTLE WHITE DOVE.

Little White Dove is a busy little person because she is learning to help mother with her many tasks. In the morning she puts on her pretty striped dress with its bead trimming and follows big sister down to the spring. She can balance a jar of water on her head and carry it up the rocky trail. She is careful not to spill or waste any water, for water is very precious in a dry country.

The hardest of a pueblo mother's tasks is to grind corn. She kneels on the ground before a stone bowl called a metate. With another stone she rubs the corn into meal. She sings as she works, keeping time to the rubbing. Often Little White Dove takes a turn at the grinding.

The family baking is done in a clay oven outside the house. The oven is round like a large clay bowl turned upside down. Little White Dove helps build a fire of brush in the oven. Mother rakes out the coals and slips in the loaves. She hangs a sheepskin over the door. In an hour or so the bread comes out, nicely baked.

Little White Dove likes to watch her mother mould beautiful jars of clay. She takes a piece of clay in her own hands and tries to make a little jar. She cannot paint as pretty a design as her mother, but she is delighted when her own little jar comes out of the firing round and whole.

Little White Dove likes to go with her mother to gather willow for the baskets that she weaves. She tries her own small brown hand at basket making, too.

Little White Dove's father and the other men of the pueblo plant the corn and wheat and take care of it with the help of the boys of the family. The men weave blankets and make moccasins.

As you see, a great deal of work goes on in the pueblo, but the children have time for play, too. Sometimes Little Chipmunk, son of the doll-maker, comes riding across the canyon on his gray burro with the present of a doll. Little White Dove's black eyes shine with delight, although you might not think the doll very pretty. It is made of painted cottonwood and feathers. It is made to look like the kachinas.

The kachinas are the men who ask the spirits to bring rain. Rain makes the corn and other crops grow so that there is plenty for everybody to eat. The kachinas, dressed in fine costumes, dance and sing. That is their way of praying to the spirits. After this dance, the dolls are given to the little girls, bows and arrows to the boys, and gifts of fruit to both.

The boys of the pueblo have their own fun. They shoot at targets or play at war with their bows and arrows. At evening, they like to go into the corral where the burros are driven for the night and play with the patient little beasts.

Little White Dove still knows only Indian ways, although some of the boys and girls go to the Government school nearby and others are sent to boarding school.

These shy brown-faced children of the pueblos seldom have to be punished. Perhaps that is because they keep so busy. Aren't you proud that these well-behaved, helpful little folks live in our own country?

LITTLE FOLKS WITHOUT A COUNTRY

Some summer evening, when you were driving in the country, you may have heard the sound of laughing, singing and fiddling that seemed to come from the next pasture. As you drew nearer, you caught a glimpse of a group of people gathered around a fire. The light of the flames showed faces darker than those of any summer camper.

Perhaps a woman in a wide skirt and a brightly embroidered shawl came out to your car and asked if she might tell your mother's fortune. A little black-eyed baby peeped over the woman's shoulder from her nest in the shawl.

"They are gypsies," mother and father told you.

"And who are gypsies and where did they come from?" you asked.

These were hard questions, for nobody really knows the answer to them. Most people think that they came from India, a big country in Asia. But nobody knows. At any rate, they have wandered over most of the world. There is hardly a country that has not a brightly painted gypsy van. Here in America the van has become an automobile.

No matter how a gypsy travels, he must keep on the move. He does not care that he has no comfortable house or fine furniture. He much prefers a chilly tent or a crowded van. It is easy to fold up a tent or hitch the horses to the van and be off when he is tired of one place.

Gypsy boys and girls enjoy all this moving just as much as their parents do. As soon as a gypsy child is too big to be carried on his mother's back, he is expected to look out for himself, and he does. Nobody tells him when to go to bed, or not to be late to breakfast.

Perhaps you think that would be fun. But how would you like it, if darkness had come on you and you were miles from your mother and father and your little white bed? Or if it was breakfast time and there was no breakfast in sight?

Little Taro does not sit down and cry. He climbs into a hen-coop or a barn and curls up and goes to sleep. In the morning he begs a fat chicken from the farmer's wife. I am afraid that sometimes he takes it without even asking.

Then he sets out to find his father and mother. He does not know where they are, but he does know how to look for them. Gypsies leave here and there little guiding marks to show which direction they have taken. They put two twigs or leaves together in a certain way. This guide is called a patteran. Every four-year-old gypsy child knows a patteran. Very soon father, mother and children meet. A fire is kindled. Taro's chicken is roasted and breakfast is ready.

Then the family separate for the day. Children start off to explore and beg. Mother goes to the village to tell fortunes.

Big Taro, who is little Taro's father, walks slowly along with another member of the family—Ivan, the great brown bear. Ivan came from the mountains of Russia. Big Taro has tamed him and taught him how to dance. Big Taro with a troop of village children following, may lead him back to the camp where the wagons were left.

He brings out a big painted tub and tucks his fiddle under his chin. At the sound of his lively tune, the big brown bear begins to dance. He hops and turns and waves his paws. The village children shout with delight and watch the wonderful bear as long as their pennies hold out. Often Big Taro takes his bear to the village square to perform.

Gypsies like Taro's family may be seen in Roumania today. There are three hundred thousand gypsies in this little country of Europe. Such gypsies usually travel in families. Some gypsies travel in companies of from twelve to fifty or so.

Hungary is another European country where there are many gypsies. In Hungary some gypsies have settled down.

Other gypsies may settle down for a little while, but with the first breath of soft spring air, they give the vans a fresh coat of bright paint and off they go.

It is a big day for the children of the countries in the south of Europe when the gypsies come to town. Gypsies are as good as a circus to them. They gather around their camping ground and watch the men making sieves, saddles or plaiting baskets. They listen to the fiddling and to the songs that go from lip to lip. If there is one thing that a gypsy loves next to his freedom, it is music.

Perhaps we cannot like all the ways of gypsy boys and girls. At any rate, we do like to see them gay and happy, fond of music and the big outdoors.

THE BIG BROWN BEAR BEGINS TO DANCE.

LITTLE FOLKS FROM THE SOUTH SEAS

Far away in the big ocean called the Pacific, there are hundreds and hundreds of islands: big islands, medium-sized islands and islands so tiny that there is not room for even one house on them. Some of the islands were made in a very strange way. They were made by tiny coral animals, the same little creatures that gave you the pink corals for your necklace.

When these animals die, they leave behind their gritty skeletons. Morsel by morsel the skeletons pile up to make coral rocks. After a very long time the rocks grew big enough to be the homes of many brown-skinned boys and girls.

The house where these two little islanders live has a peaked roof with a thatch of cocoanut fibres. Its one room has a platform of stone for a floor. Fiu and Aretemoi sleep on mats woven of cocoanut fibre. There is no other furniture in the house.

Close by the house stands a cluster of cocoanut trees with their tall slender trunks and tufts of plumey leaves at the tops. Fiu's and Aretemoi's people know that this tree is their best friend. Fiu and the older boys climb up the slender trunks like monkeys and gather the ripe nuts. They drink the milky juice and eat the sweet white meat. You know how good cocoanut tastes on the icing of your birthday cake.

Fiu's father and the other men cut the cocoanut shells into dishes. His mother weaves mats from the fibres. The cocoanuts that they cannot use are cut in halves and the meat is dried in the hot sun. Fiu's father sells his copra, as the sun-dried cocoanut is called, to the traders who ship it to other countries. Some of the oil used in our soaps and face creams comes to us from the cocoanuts dried by Fiu's people.

Fiu and Aretemoi live on one of these coral islands. Their island is shaped a little like a doughnut. The island itself is the hole. All around it is a circle of dazzling blue waters called a lagoon. A ring of coral reefs keeps the angry waves of the ocean from the calm water inside. An island like this is called an atoll.

Fiu and Aretemoi have brown skin, black eyes and jet black hair. Their bodies are graceful and strong. They learned to swim as soon as they could walk. It is not hard for them to keep clean with such a big bathtub as the lagoon close by. After a bath they like to rub their brown bodies with oil from the cocoanut and make their skin glisten and shine.

Fiu and Aretemoi are not troubled with many clothes. In so warm a country as theirs they do not need them. Around their waists they drape a piece of bright colored printed cloth. Aretemoi's grandmother used to make her dress by pounding the bark of a tree into a rough kind of cloth. She called her dress a tapa cloth. Now it is easier to buy cotton from the traders than to make the cloth from the bark.

Aretemoi loves flowers. She often fastens them in her jet black hair. There are many beautiful flowers in the jungle. When she goes to gather them, she hears the chattering of the parakeets and sees the flicker of the bright plumage of the fruit pigeon among the trees. Fiu likes to go poking among the rocks to catch the bright colored fish.

Let us see what Aretemoi and Fiu are going to have for dinner. Their mother has laid fresh banana leaves on the ground for a cloth. They will have some of the fish that Fiu has caught. Often they eat them raw. Instead of potatoes they have roasted taro root. Very often Aretemoi helps her mother to pound the taro root into a gray kind of paste called poi poi, which makes a rather sour tasting dish. You will not see any bread like ours on their table. Their bread grows on a tree and is called breadfruit.

Fiu and Aretemoi think it fun to go out on the smooth waters of the lagoon. Their father has two wooden canoes fastened a little distance apart by poles. Such canoes are very steady. Fiu and Aretemoi like to look down into the clear water. They seem to see a beautiful garden of many colored flowers and ferns. But they are really the branches of coral that have grown into odd shapes. Strange bright fish dart in and out among the coral branches.

There are oysters, too, on the floor of the lagoon, and Fiu and Aretemoi know that in some of them there are pearls. Sometimes a grain of sand or a tiny sea animal gets inside an oyster shell. It troubles the oyster and to make itself more comfortable the oyster coats the grain with layer after layer of the same material as its shell. Finally it makes the beautiful round thing we call a pearl.

FIU AND ARETEMOI LIVE A HAPPY, CAREFREE LIFE.

Fine pearls are worth a great deal of money. At certain times of the year Aretemoi's father and other islanders go fishing for pearls to sell. They go out in canoes, two men together. One drops a weighted rope. The other puts water goggles on his eyes, a clasp like a clothes-pin on his nose, and long leather thimbles on his fingers to protect them from the sharp coral rocks. A stone is tied to his feet to help him sink. He takes some deep breaths and lets himself down the rope. The stone is pulled up when he gets to the bottom. Then he fills his basket with oysters and comes up the rope, leaving the basket to be drawn up afterward. Sometimes pearl fishers dive without ropes.

The fisher slips his hand very carefully into the oyster shell to find the pearl. Then he lets the oyster down gradually into the water so that it may live to make another pearl. Some pearl fishers let the oysters die.

Diving for pearls is very dangerous work. A diver can stay under water not much longer than a minute. The water pressing down upon him may make him deaf or unconscious. Besides a shark or a great devil-fish may attack him or a giant eel wind itself about his body.

The South Seas have their dangers, to be sure, but Fiu and Aretemoi live a happy carefree life there, in that land of fruits and flowers. They would not exchange it for yours.

LITTLE FOLKS FROM THE LAND OF THE SOMBRERO

No, Manuel has not borrowed his father's hat. It is his very own. He does not think it a bit too large, for Manuel lives in Mexico, the land of big hats.

Mexico is a country that will seem as strange to you as if it lay across the ocean instead of right next to the southwestern part of our own country. A three days' journey in a Pullman car from the northern part of our country will carry you to this foreign land.

On the map, Mexico looks like a big cornucopia. If you should cut up our own United States into four parts, one of the parts would be as large as Mexico. There are only about fourteen million people in Mexico.

In Mexico you would find nearly everybody speaking the Spanish language. This is because long ago the Spaniards took the country away from the Indians they found there. For three hundred years they ruled over the country. Then Mexico decided to govern itself. It has not been easy work. There have been many revolutions and the fighting still goes on.

Some of the people of Mexico are pure Indians of the same race the Spanish conquerors found there. Some are the descendants of Spanish fathers and Indian mothers. The rest are Spanish or people from other countries.

Even if Mexico is only a fourth as large as the United States, there is too much of it to be seen in one trip. How different the country will look to you as you go from one part to another.

Manuel lives up in the northern part, on a big plantation called a hacienda. It is owned by a very wealthy man who has hundreds of men working for him. Some of them raise grain and others care for sheep and cattle. Manuel helps tend the goats. He often rides about on a little donkey, called a burro, to keep them from straying away. When he grows bigger he will be a real cowboy.

Manuel's hat seems to be the biggest part of him. He calls it a sombrero. He is very proud of it. A Mexican thinks he must have a fine hat no matter how poor the rest of his clothes are. Often his hat costs from twenty-five to over a hundred dollars. Sombreros are made of felt or straw. The crown is high and peaked. The brim is sometimes as wide as your foot-ruler is long. It is often embroidered with gold and silver thread.

Next to his sombrero, Manuel thinks most of his serape. The serape is a gaily striped blanket with a hole to let the head through. In Mexico it takes the place of an overcoat. Manuel wears clothes of coarse cotton under his serape.

His mother's dress is of cotton, too, made with short sleeves. She never wears a hat or shoes. Out of doors, her head is covered with a brown shawl called a rebosa. Sometimes her shawl is arranged so as to make a pouch for Manuel's baby sister.

If Manuel's mother should invite you to dinner, do not expect any bread and butter. You would have instead, freshly baked tortillas or corn cakes. You would think them rather tasteless, but Manuel's mother took a great deal of trouble to make them. Kneeling on the floor she ground the corn between two stones for many hours. Then she patted the paste into cakes and baked them.

MANUEL'S HAT SEEMS TO BE THE BIGGEST PART OF HIM.

Let us say good-bye to Manuel and his mother and leave the dry plains with their prickly cactuses for another part of Mexico. Before we come to Mexico City, the capital of the country, there are miles and miles of great stiff plants growing far higher than your head. You may have seen a single plant like these in the center of a wide lawn and called it a century plant. Mexicans call it the maguey and they think a great deal of it. No wonder, for the maguey gives them all sorts of useful things, from a needle to a roof for the house. In fact, the maguey is sometimes called the thread and needle plant. If a little Mexican girl needs to mend her doll's dress she pushes one of the long thorns along the edges of the leaves of the maguey back into its sheath and then pulls it out. With it come tiny fibers. If she twists this thorn-needle just right, the fibers twine together to make a strong thread.

The Mexicans dry the leaves of the maguey to make roofs for their houses. They make ropes from the fibers of the leaves and braid them into mats for tables or chairs. They make a fire of the part of the plant which cannot be used for anything else and cook the roots over it, which they use for food.

But most of all, the Mexican grows the maguey for its juice. He calls it "honey-water," and from it makes a drink called pulque.

The people of Mexico take the juice from the plant in a very odd way. Just before the plant is ready to blossom, they cut out the center of the stem. A hollow is left as big around as a washbowl. The sweet sap runs into this hollow. Two or three times a day little Alphonso comes with his father to get it. Alphonso's father puts one end of a long, thin gourd in the bowl of sap, then with his lips at the other end, he draws up the sap into the gourd. Then he pours the sap into a pigskin and hangs it over his shoulders, or carries it away in jars on a donkey's back.

As you leave the maguey plantation behind, you come into Mexico City. This beautiful city, like every other Mexican town, has a park called a plaza in its center. There is a bandstand where the people come evenings and Sunday mornings to listen to the music they love. A very large and beautiful cathedral faces the plaza. There are many fine churches in Mexico.

The houses with their high stone walls and heavy iron bars look very gloomy. Once there were many robbers in Mexico, so the houses had to be barred. Inside the huge door how different everything looks! The house is built around a courtyard called a patio. There are trees, flowering vines, a fountain and birds singing in cages. Carmen and Miguel, the children of the family, play in the garden. The grown-ups watch the fun from the porch around the patio.

Of course many Mexican children do not have such fine homes as Carmen and Miguel. The poorer people live in square, windowless huts of adobe or sun-dried brick. These huts are not very pretty but they are cooler in summer and warmer in winter than wooden houses.

Carmen and Miguel ask you to stay and share in their Christmas celebration. At Christmas time they march through the patio carrying lighted candles and singing. The best fun is the breaking of the pinate. The pinate is a great jar filled with candies, nuts and toys. The jar is covered with bright paper to make it look like a big doll or a bird. The children are blindfolded and take their turn at hitting at the jar. When at last it breaks, what a scrambling there is for the toys!

You would enjoy this frolic, but I am sure you would not exchange your own Christmas tree for a pinate.

LITTLE FOLKS OF THE LAND OF THE WHITE ELEPHANT

You may think that stars and stripes make the finest flag in the world. But on the other side of the globe there are boys and girls who are sure that a white elephant on a red background is the prettiest thing in flags.

These boys and girls live in Siam, called sometimes the Land of the White Elephant. It is rather a small country to the south of big China. It is only about five times as large as our own state of Kentucky, and has nine or ten million people.

The boys and girls of the Land of the White Elephant have yellow or brown skins and rather flat faces with high cheek bones. Their hair is straight and black and their twinkling eyes are black, too.

Siam is such a hot country that its people, except in cities, wear as few clothes as possible. Chua, the little son of a rice farmer, twists a strip of colored cloth around his waist to make his trousers. The upper part of his body is bare, but his mother and sister wear scarves.

Chua lives in a house built high on stilts to keep it out of the water when the heavy rains flood his country. Chua's cousin Mee lives in a floating house. In many parts of Siam, the rivers and canals are the streets. Thousands of people live in houseboats built on rafts, or in real boats. The city of Bangkok however, has some of the finest paved streets in the Far East. Mee has a little boat of his own and does the family errands in it. Of course he can swim like a fish. When he was only a baby, his mother fastened a tin float under his arms and let him bob up and down in the water like a cork.

There is very little furniture either in the land house of Chua or in the water house of Mee. Only a few mats and a charcoal stove.

Chua's father, like many other Siamese, raises rice for a living. The people of Siam grow so much rice that everybody in the kingdom could have a pound and then there would be some left over.

When it comes ploughing time, Chua helps harness the water buffalo to the wooden plough. The water buffalo is a fierce-looking beast with long curling horns. He is not really ugly. Indeed, Chua's little sister can ride him. He will work patiently for his master, if only every now and then he can get into the water and cool off.

Chua's father stores his rice and grain in a queer sort of little barn built high up on an island to keep it out of the water and away from any prowling animals. This storehouse has decorations that look like water buffaloes. Chua's people believe these queer figures will keep evil spirits away. When the rice is ready to sell, Chua carries a load of it down the river in his father's boat.

Chua's house and storehouse are built of teak wood. There are great forests of teak in Siam. In fact, Chua's country grows more of this wood than any other country in the world. Teak wood has so much oil in it that it does not rot in water. It is just the right kind of wood for making houses that have to stand in the water half of the time.

Men cut down the teak wood trees in the forest, and elephants carry the logs to the streams to be floated down to the sawmills. Friend Elephant can pick up a log in his trunk and carry it long distances. He can also pile the logs neatly. He must do his job in his own way, or he refuses to work.

Leam, another little Siamese boy, lives near the teak forest. His father is a mahout, or elephant driver. Sometimes he lets Leam ride his elephant down to the river for a cool bath.

MEE HAS A LITTLE BOAT OF HIS OWN.

Perhaps you are wondering why the country of Siam has a white elephant on its flag. Leam's elephant, like the rest of the working elephants, have leathery skins, the color of your slate. These elephants are much like those you see in a circus. Once in a while an elephant is found with a skin of lighter gray. Such an elephant is called white. He is really a sick elephant.

Some Siamese believe that the soul of a great person has gone into the body of the white elephant. All the white elephants that were found used to be given to the king.

The white elephant had a palace all his own with robes of silk and satin embroidered with precious jewels. His tusks were bound with gold, and he had slaves to wait on him. Poor elephant, he would have been far happier tramping in the forest. Nowadays the king keeps only a few white elephants.

You may think it would be better to call Siam the Land of the Gray Elephant instead of the White Elephant. Surely the great faithful slate-colored beast does a big share of the country's work.

LITTLE FOLKS FROM THE LAND OF THE REINDEER

When you wake up and find the sun shining, you know that it is day and time to get up. But the little folks of Lapland, for a month or two in summer can see the sun shine at midnight, if they happen to be awake. In winter for the same length of time, they never see the sun at all. This is because they live so very far north. Lapland is a name that is given to the parts of Norway, Sweden and Finland that are nearest the great cold Arctic Ocean.

To have daylight all the time in the summer, you may think would be rather good fun. But how would you like winter days without any sunlight at all? Thorkild and Gudrun, like other little Lapps, are quite used to finding their way around in the dark. Besides, in Lapland, it is not as dark as night is with us. The stars shine very

OFTEN THEY RIDE ON THEIR OWN REINDEER.

brightly. Then, too, often strange waves of light dart across the sky; sometimes they are all the colors of the rainbow, sometimes only a silvery white. They are called Northern Lights.

When Thorkild and Gudrun, our little Lapp friends, were tiny babies, their father gave them each a reindeer for their very own. Their father owns over a thousand reindeer. He is richer than some of his neighbors, but, even a poor Lapp may have as many as twenty-five reindeer.

In winter all the food the reindeer can find is a sort of moss that they dig up from under the snow. When the reindeer eat up the moss in one place, they have to move on to another. The family that owns them has to go along too. It happens, then, that Thorkild and Gudrun are moving very often. To be sure, their father keeps a storehouse in a Lapp village, and sometimes they come there to visit friends who do not wander about. Then the children go to school.

When Thorkild and Gudrun's family are following the reindeer, they live in a tent. The tent is covered with reindeer skin or a thick woolen cloth. Hay spread with reindeer skins does duty for carpet, chairs and beds. The children's mother builds a fire on a circle of flat stones in the middle of the tent. The smoke is supposed to go out of a hole in the top of the tent.

Gudrun helps her mother cook the meals over the smoky fire. There is always plenty of strong coffee made with melted snow. The grown-ups use reindeer milk in their coffee, and the little folks can have all the milk they want to drink. They smack their lips over a stew of reindeer meat. They never have to be coaxed to eat their spinach, because they have no vegetables.

You can imagine there is not much room in a Lapp tent with grown-ups, children and dogs all mixed up together. Where do you suppose they keep the babies? They strap them into their shoe-shaped cradles and hang them up out of the way.

Baby, in his moss-lined cradle, wears no clothes except his blanket, but Thorkild and Gudrun, who tumble about in the snow all day long, need very warm clothing. Their mother makes it, except for their woolen under clothing, from reindeer skin. Both Thorkild and Gudrun wear leather trousers tucked into their soft high boots. They stuff their boots with hay and dry them every night. Lapp children know that they must keep their feet dry or Jack Frost will nip them. They love to wear bright colored scarves and boot lacings.

Gudrun's mother is a very busy person. She makes the clothes for the whole family; boots, coats, gloves, as well as many garments to sell. She sews them with thread made from reindeer sinew. She does all the cooking and looks after the reindeer.

The Lapp father has a hard job when he breaks in a three-year-old reindeer to draw a sleigh. He coaxes the young reindeer with salt, which it loves, until he is near enough to slip a collar over its head. Then the fun begins, for the reindeer is a wild creature and never likes a harness.

Even when the reindeer is supposed to be thoroughly broken, a ride behind him is exciting. A Lapp sleigh is a little like a boat. It runs on one runner like a keel. As the reindeer dashes over the snow at a terrific pace, the sleigh rocks from side to side. Thorkild and Gudrun had many a spill before they learned how to hold on. Their faces are hard and rosy from many tumbles in the snow. One of the wildest rides is when they and their friends go over the mountains to the villages to sell the things they have made from reindeer skins, and to buy coffee and other provisions for the next winter.

Thorkild and Gudrun can walk quickly on skis and never lose their balance. Lapp skis are covered with reindeer hide. Often they ride on their own reindeer, sitting on their necks behind their big branching antlers.

At Christmas time they have a party. Everybody brings a candle to hang on a big spruce tree. Then there are merry games around the tree. So you see that the cold doesn't prevent these hardy little Lapps from having plenty of fun.

LITTLE FOLKS FROM THE LAND OF MANY PEOPLE

Away over on the other side of the globe, just about opposite to us, if you could dig straight through the earth, is a country even larger than our own great country. It is a quarter larger, in fact, for it has over four million, two hundred and fifty thousand square miles.

It has more miles and ever and ever so many more people than we. About four hundred and fifty million of them. It is hard to think of so many people, isn't it? Just try to imagine all the people in our United States, in Canada up to the north of us, in the big continent of South America to the south of us, in the great continent of Africa on the other side of the world, all put together. China has as many people as that.

That means that about a quarter of the people in the world live in China. China is so crowded with people that they have to work harder for a living than we do. No other people in the world work so hard.

Let us see some of the ways in which this country is different from our own. Chinese boys and girls as well as their elders do not look in the least like you or your fathers and mothers. That is because they belong to a different race called the Yellow race.

Their skins are cream-color and their bright black eyes slant. Their hair is very black and very straight. The girls wear it cut short over the forehead with the rest rolled up on the top of the head. It used to be the fashion for Chinese men and boys to keep their hair long and braid it in a long plait called a queue, but nowadays most of them cut it short.

Let us make friends with some Chinese boys and girls. Then we shall see how very different their clothes are from your own. Here is Chan Lee. He wears long loose trousers of blue cotton and a loose coat of the same material. On his head he has a big round straw hat like a parasol to shade him from the hot sun. When he is at work in the fields picking tea leaves you can scarcely see Chan Lee for his hat. When the tea leaves gathered by Chan Lee are dried, they are packed and sent across the Pacific Ocean to us, and to other countries. Some of the best tea in the world comes from China. China was the first country to use tea.

THE HOLIDAY THEY LIKE BEST OF ALL IS NEW YEAR'S DAY.

Most of our little Chinese friends, like Chan Lee, are clothed in cotton. China raises a great deal of cotton so that cotton clothes do not cost much. When the weather is cold, a Chinese mother puts a padded cotton suit on her little boy. If it is very cold she puts another on top of that. If he isn't warm enough, then she adds still another until the little fellow looks like a stuffed rag doll. He can scarcely move he has on so many clothes. Houses in China, even those of rich people, are not heated like ours with furnaces, so that people must put on many clothes to keep warm.

Here are Ling-Wu and his sister Charming Flower. They do not have to work like Chan Lee because their father is a rich silk merchant. Charming Flower wears long yellow satin trousers and a loose jacket of yellow and red, embroidered in a fancy pattern. She has gay red satin slippers on her feet. When Charming Flower's grandmother was a little girl she had her feet bound tightly to make them small. The pain was almost more than she could bear. Nowadays few Chinese ladies keep up this silly custom.

Ling-Wu has a beautiful coat of purple silk trimmed with blue and orange, and trousers of blue silk. On his head he has a little round purple cap with a button on the top. He keeps his cap on in the house. He wears white socks. His shoes are made of black felt with the soles painted white.

Everybody who can afford it in China wears a great deal of silk and satin. The busy little silkworms of China spin enough silk for half the people of the world to use. Very likely the silk of your daddy's necktie was spun by a tiny silk worm over in China.

If we follow Ling-Wu and Charming Flower into their house, we shall see that Chinese houses are in most ways very different from our own. Their house stands back from the street in a large yard surrounded by a wall. There are other houses in the yard belonging to Ling-Wu's uncles and their families.

There are many rooms in the house and some of them look out on beautiful gardens. There are fountains in the gardens with bright colored goldfish swimming in them.

Ling-Wu and his family have tables and chairs much like our own. Most of the furniture is made of black wood beautifully carved. Some of the chairs are of wickerwork.

I'm sure you would not like a bed like Ling-Wu's. Around the outside wall of his bedroom runs a ledge of brick. Ling-Wu wraps his bed clothes around him and sleeps on a piece of matting laid on top of this ledge. He has a hard block of wood for a pillow. There are pipes under the ledge, and in cold weather a fire is made in them to keep the beds warm during the night.

Dinner time comes while we are in Ling-Wu's house. It is lucky that you do not have to eat. You would have a hard time getting along without knives and forks. Ling-Wu and his family eat with chopsticks which look like large bone knitting needles. We notice that there are no table cloths or napkins. After the meal everyone wipes his face and hands with a cloth dipped in a bowl of hot water.

As for the food, it is not like ours, but it is very good indeed. The Chinese are excellent cooks. There is plenty of rice, for Ling-Wu would not know what to make of a meal without rice. In fact a Chinaman is very likely to speak of his breakfast as "morning rice," his lunch as "noon rice" and his supper as "evening rice."

In a rich family like Ling-Wu's, there are plenty of good things to eat besides rice. There are pork and chicken, duck and many odd vegetables. There are sweetmeats, dried watermelon seeds, red persimmons and many other fruits. The meat and vegetables are cut up into small pieces before they are cooked. In that form they can be eaten without forks. When Ling-Wu's father is giving a party he sometimes serves a soup made out of birds' nests or sharks' fins. Delicious tea served in cups without handles with the saucer placed on top, goes with every meal.

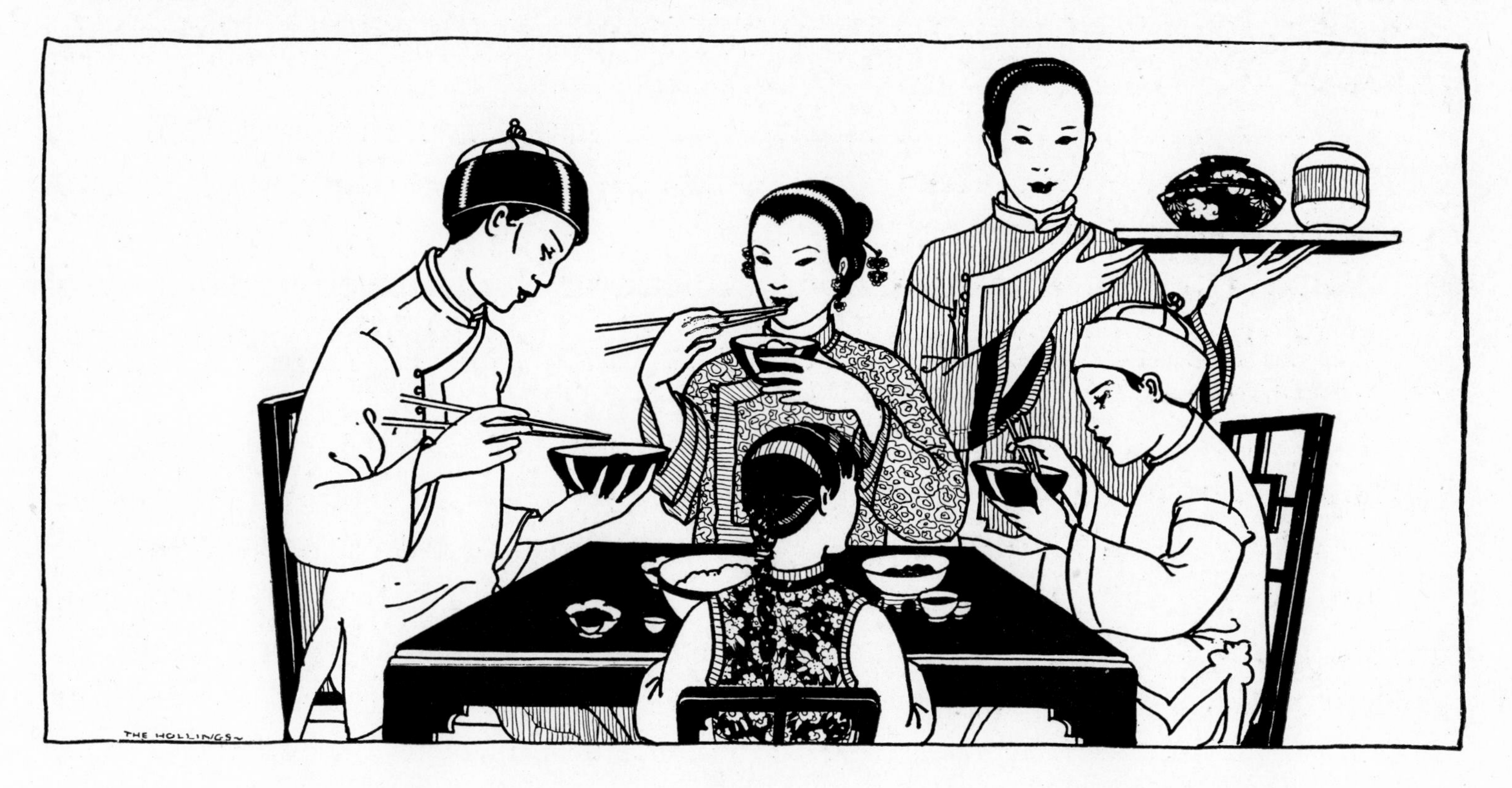

Of course the houses in China are not all as fine as Ling-Wu's. Many are only huts with thatched roofs of mud and reeds. In the large cities most of the houses are only one story high and are crowded close together. In the poorer houses there is only a little rough furniture. Boys and girls who live in such houses live mostly on rice with a few vegetables and fish.

And now let us look into a Chinese schoolroom. You will think the books very strange. The children begin on the last page and read forward. The lines on the pages run up and down and not across like ours. Ling-Wu does not have to learn his letters, for there are no A B C's in the Chinese language. But he has a harder task than that. Every one of the strange-looking marks in his books stands for a word. There are thousands of them to learn instead of just twenty-six letters.

He must learn to write them, too. He does not write with a pen, but he paints the letters with a brush. He must hold the brush exactly as the teacher shows him.

Ling-Wu does his number work on a counting box called an abacus. He pushes little colored balls back and forth on its wires and solves his sums in that way.

Not so very long ago Chinese girls were not sent to school at all. Chinese boys had to learn by heart many difficult books filled with the sayings of a wise man of ancient times called Confucius. They had one schoolbook that had three thousand rules for good manners, and another full of stories about Chinese people who became famous because they were so good to their parents.

They used to shout their lessons at the top of their lungs, and still do in some of the country schools. But nowadays almost everywhere in China boys and girls have much the same kind of lessons as you do.

Chinese boys and girls have to study hard, but they have a great many holidays. The one they like best of all is New Year's Day. They celebrate it on the first new moon of the year. On New Year's Day all the boys and girls call themselves one year older. They run about the streets shouting good wishes to one another.

New Year's Eve is as noisy in China as it is in New York City. Gongs are striking, bells are ringing and trumpets blowing. Firecrackers are popping everywhere and the streets are littered with their red papers. There are beautiful fireworks making pictures of birds, animals and fish with their flames. The Chinese knew about fireworks many long years before we did. It was they who first discovered how to make gunpowder. The firecrackers you set off on the fourth of July were probably made by a Chinaman. He can make several thousand a day. He receives only a few cents for all his patient hand work.

As with us, New Year's Eve in China is a time for making good resolutions. You might hear a boy shouting in the street, "I want to sell my lazy ways."

Just before midnight, everybody quiets down. They go into the house and bow before the tablets that are kept in memory of their relatives who lived many years before them. The Chinese worship their ancestors. Every few days they put presents of food before the tablets and burn incense.

New Year's morning is gay again. The children have gifts wrapped in red paper to bring good luck. Such wonderful things they find in the red paper: dolls with everything they need to set up housekeeping, tops, kites and dancing toys of every sort.

In our peep at this great country, you have found many things that seem strange to you. Years ago China was even more different from our own country than it is now. The Chinese liked to do as their fathers and grandfathers did before them. They did not like to have people from other countries try to change their ways. But gradually they did make changes. Today there are railroads and automobiles as in our own country, though a well-to-do Chinaman may still go out for an airing in a sedan chair carried by two men. One of the greatest changes is the way in which the country is governed. Now China has a president at its head just as we do.

LITTLE FOLKS FROM THE FAR NORTH

What are those furry little creatures in the snow? From out their hoods peer slanting black eyes set in chubby brown faces. And how they laugh! They are not wild animals but Tatuk and Too-kee, a little Eskimo boy and girl.

These merry little people live far away in the frozen North, above the Arctic Circle. It would take a long, long time to reach their country by steamer, and the boat might be frozen in on the way. So you will have to content yourself with visiting them in books.

THESE MERRY LITTLE PEOPLE LIVE FAR AWAY IN THE FROZEN NORTH.

It is winter—and such a cold winter—except for a few months of the year in this far northern country. Tatuk and Too-kee have to wear plenty of warm clothes and eat the kind of food that keeps them warm. They dress in fur and that is why they look so much like little wild creatures.

Too-kee's outside coat is made with the fur turned outward. It is called a parka. This coat once belonged to a polar bear. Too-kee's father killed the bear. Her mother peeled off the skin and dried it. Then she chewed the skin until it was soft enough to pierce with her bone needle. Too-kee's inside suit is made of bird skins. She has pockets in her outside coat and in her fur boots. She keeps her doll in one. Her father carved it for her from a walrus tusk. He killed the walrus by throwing a harpoon into his side.

Tatuk is dressed much the same as his sister. His inside clothes and stockings are made of the skin of a young reindeer, the fur side next to his skin. Tatuk and Too-kee in their suits furnished by the seal, the bear and other good beasts and birds of the North are warm and cosy in weather colder than the coldest you could ever imagine. Too-kee's mother has a long bag of fur on the back of her parka. This is where she carries her baby. In his little fur shirt and cap he is snug and warm in this soft nest.

What well-heated houses these little folks must need for so cold a country! You will be surprised to hear that they often live in houses made of snow! Tatuk's house looks like half of a great snowball tossed down by a giant. It is called an igloo. His father built it of cakes of snow. The front door is a cake of ice. The front hall is a long narrow tunnel in the snow. The children have to crawl on their hands and knees to get in. The window is a piece of skin from the inside of a whale.

It is so warm inside that the family throw off most of their clothes. Yet there is no stove, only a big stone bowl full of burning oil. For a wick, this lamp-stove has a ring of dried moss. The flame makes a great smoke and the faces of Tatuk, Too-kee and the rest of the family are very smutty and dirty.

The Eskimo mother cooks the meals over this odd lamp-stove. When the father spears a seal that has come up out of the water to breathe, he drags it into the house. The mother cuts it up and boils it in a pot full of melted snow.

Tatuk and Too-kee eat with their fingers. They like the fat pieces of meat best of all. Fat tastes as good to them as candy or ice-cream to you. They need to eat plenty of fat to help keep them warm. These Eskimo friends do not like salt in their food. They often eat fish and in the short summer they have birds and wild berries to eat.

Across one side of the house is a ledge of snow. It is covered with soft skins of seals and polar bears. At night the family use this ledge for a bed. In the daytime it is their sofa.

Eskimos have to move when they have caught all the wild animals near their home. They can build a snow house so easily in only a few hours that they do not mind leaving the old one. In the short summers, they make tents called topeks of sealskins.

Of course there are no automobiles in Eskimo land. There are not even any horses or roads. When Tatuk's father wants to go on a journey to see where there is good hunting, he harnesses his dogs to a sled. He cracks his long whip and the huskies go racing over the ice and snow like the wind.

Sometimes Tatuk's father lets him go fishing in his boat. The boat is a queer sort of canoe made of wood and covered with skins. It is called a kayak. Tatuk sits in the middle and sends his kayak shooting through the water with a double paddle. A cover of skins comes tight around his waist. He can turn over and over with the boat so quickly that no water gets in.

Up in Eskimo land the sun behaves very strangely, or so it would seem to us. But Tatuk and Too-kee are not at all surprised when in winter the sun goes down at two o'clock in the afternoon and doesn't get up again until ten the next morning. Yet it does not grow very dark in the northland.

It is not winter all of the time in Eskimo land. For a few months summer comes, and then Mr. Sun has to work overtime. He is on duty all but two or three hours of the day. No wonder the snow melts fast and the plants begin to spring up.

Tatuk's father sells the fine skins of the polar bear, seals, and foxes he catches to the men who come on trading ships. These men bring him knives, axes, beads, mirrors, and many other things which he likes very much.

Tatuk and Too-kee do not go to school as you do, but they have to learn a good many things. Too-kee learns how to cure skins and to sew them into clothes for her doll. Tatuk learns how to shoot with a bow and arrow, how to watch for seals and to spear them, how to drive a dog team, and to manage a kayak.

These little people never complain of the cold. They love to hunt and fish and to tumble about in the snow. They have as much fun in their way as you do in yours.